PRAISE FOR JACQUELINE PIRTLE

Jacqueline takes you always directly to what you are ready to see or experience.

— LONGTIME CLIENT AND READER

It is liberating to face your own blocks and to be finally free of the weight that they have caused for many years. And while for me the changes I'm experiencing are noticeable and real, I still feel like myself. Just a more sure self.

— LONGTIME CLIENT AND READER

Jacqueline's guidance is so in-tune with what is happening mentally for you.

— LONGTIME CLIENT AND READER

JACQUELINE PIRTLE

What.
If.

Turning your IFs into it IS!

THE EXTENDED EDITION

COPYRIGHT

Copyright © 2021 Jacqueline Pirtle
www.FreakyHealer.com

All rights reserved. No part of this book may be reproduced or transmitted in any form or by any means, electronic or mechanical, including photocopying, recording, or by any information storage and retrieval system without the written permission of the publisher, except where permitted by law.

ISBN-13: 978-1-955059-04-6

Publisher: Freaky Healer

Editor-in-chief: Zoe Pirtle
All-round Support: Mitch Pirtle

Book cover design by Kingwood Creations kingwoodcreations.com

Author photo courtesy of Lionel Madiou madious.com

I want to let you know that all my books and holistic practitioner work together are a wholesome system, supporting you to live a more conscious, mindful, and happier life.

However, I made it so you can receive the benefit of living more joyously solely by working through this terrific journal book, while also experiencing the full satisfaction in continuing on to the next journal of this series—not to mention the rock solid tools you get by reading any of my other books or adding in my podcast **The Daily Freak**. Either way, I know you'll love my inspirational teachings.

Find out more:
www.freakyhealer.com
Amazon Author Page
The Daily Freak Podcast

So before you dive in, I want to thank you for hopping on the magic train with me! I truly hope you enjoy **What. If.** as much as I loved writing it, and if you do, it would be wonderful if you could take a short minute and leave a review on Amazon.com and Goodreads.com as soon as you can.

Your kind feedback helps other readers find my books easier, and be happy faster. Consider it a happy deed for the world.

Thank you!

ACKNOWLEDGMENTS

Let's be honest here… I have a dream team!

I could not have finished this book without the help of talented, creative, high-for-life, and phenomenal professionals.

From the bottom of my heart, I want to thank Zoe Pirtle for her editorial mastery; Mitch Pirtle for his all-round support; kingwoodcreations.com for their fun and polished book cover design; and madiouART.com for an amazing photo shoot.

I'd also like to extend a huge "Thank You!" to all the fans of my work and books—I created this beautiful journal series for you.

Life is spectacular with you on my side!

Just think about it:

You have the power to imagine, think, feel, and journal yourself into a high-for-life frequency—a space where life IS believably phenomenal.

DEDICATION

*I dedicate this journal to all **what IFs** and challenge them to become **what IS**.*

INTRODUCTION

Amazing *what if-er*,

I can't even grasp how wonderful it is for me to know that you are starting to work through this 90 day journal - the extended edition - of **What.If.** Even better, no words can describe my excitement for what will change for you, and what new-ness will BE for you, because of your conscious work that you are about to embark on by hanging out with all your *what ifs*.

Seriously, have you ever wondered *what if* this or that would change, be, or happen—how different it all would be for you?

I sure have!

All *what ifs* present unlimited opportunities to become *what IS* because of the shift they initiate in anyone entertaining thinking about them, feeling, visualizing and imagining them, and also using the words *what if*—not to mention the possible manifestations when at the same time thinking and feeling about the *what IS* that's at the other end of every *what if*.

Every *what if* has the capability to shoot you automatically into thinking of how it IS when your desires and wishes happen, when the *what if* becomes *what IS*—of course that asks of you to BE and live open to such glory.

INTRODUCTION

Sounds like a magical time to me, if your other option is to hang around in a life that does not have your deepest desires and wishes present.

Everything is energy, you, me, your *what ifs* and every *what IS*. All is the same and connected, sharing energy at all times—meaning that you and your *what ifs* and what they represent - your *what IS* - are all one and the same. Energy!

As these energies, everything and everyone vibrates in different frequencies, some are high like happiness, and some are lower like anger.

Your *what ifs* and the wished-for *what IS* are of a high value frequency, they feel good because they represent betterment, living forward, and being happier. They are your wishes, dreams, and desires! Focusing on them, dreaming about them, feeling and thinking about them and their becoming true, is a spectacular way of being and living.

However, when you put all that you have on the absence of your *what ifs* by focusing on that missing link, you are vibrating in a lower frequency because absence means "not enough," "never going to happen," "not possible for me," or "I give up." Absence also brings on feelings like sadness, weakness, anger or frustration, feelings of being un-deserving or even thoughts that this *what if* is way too big and good for you. It's like focusing on the smelly full diaper instead of enjoying the beauty of a baby.

Start thinking of your *what ifs* by focusing only on the magic of dreaming up your life and the manifestation into that *what IS*. Feel your utmost excitement and awe of everything being possible, you being deserving, and you being in charge of how your life IS and unfolds, and what's included or excluded fully.

Spending quality time with your *what ifs* shifts you into a high-for-life frequency—where all your *what ifs* are waiting to turn into your *what IS*.

In this journal you will do exactly that; hang out with your *what ifs to* become BFFs for you to BE and live the most positive

INTRODUCTION

and fulfilled life ever so that the manifestations of your dreams, wishes, and desires are possible.

Every day in this book, there is a profound *what if* scenario, inviting you to shift yourself into feeling amazing by journaling about your answers to the fitting questions—creating love, peace, happiness, appreciation, respect, gratitude, acceptance for yourself, your life, and your truth which you will share with everything and everyone.

You will become a master in manifesting, all while learning to feel better, live more consciously and mindfully, and become happier.

I say let's go and turn your *what ifs* into your *what IS* to change your life forever!

As a side note, there are a couple bonus days at the end; in case you ever find the need to do two in a day, or to keep working while you wait for the next journal in this series to arrive. I also left you a few blank *what if* pages to journal about additional wishes and dreams as they come in and up for you.

Enough chit-chat, I know you are ready, so grab your pen and have incredible fun with your *what ifs*.

Happiest,
   Jacqueline

ay 1

WHAT IF YOU would be able to turn all your *what ifs* into *what IS* with unquestionable easy-ness? What would change and what would happen for you? How different would you feel and live, and show up every day?

_____
_____
_____
_____
_____
_____
_____
_____
_____
_____
_____
_____
_____
_____
_____
_____
_____
_____
_____
_____
_____
_____

Turning your what IFs into what IS!

ay 2

WHAT IF YOU would live your full power? What would be different for you? What would happen? What does your full power feel and look like?

_____
_____
_____
_____
_____
_____
_____
_____
_____
_____
_____
_____
_____
_____
_____
_____
_____
_____
_____
_____
_____
_____

Turning your what IFs into what IS!

ay 3

WHAT IF YOU would listen to your inner being - your inner voice, your gut instinct - without ever doubting it? How different would your life be? How can you listen to your inner knowing at all times?

Turning your what IFs into what IS!

ay 4

WHAT IF YOU would blindly believe in love? What would happen for you, your loved ones, and your relationships? How will you enjoy love freely?

Turning your what IFs into what IS!

ay 5

WHAT IF YOU would make yourself and your well-feeling a priority? What wellness would grow out of that action? How would that change your physical, emotional, and spiritual health?

Turning your what IFs into what IS!

ay 6

WHAT IF YOU move on from all bad, ugly, and wrong—no matter its nature? What kind of release would that be? How will you move beyond all the gunk, and on to enjoying life freely?

___

Turning your what IFs into what IS!

ay 7

WHAT IF YOU would live without limits—and live limitless? What possibilities and opportunities would that way of living present to you? What limits are you going to shed?

Turning your what IFs into what IS!

ay 8

WHAT IF YOU would go for what you want? What would happen? How will you choose your wishes, dreams, and desires more often?

___

Turning your what IFs into what IS!

ay 9

WHAT IF YOU would smile more? What changes would that create —for you, your physical emotional and spiritual health, and also for others? How will you put a smile every once in a while?

___

Turning your what IFs into what IS!

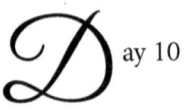 ay 10

WHAT IF YOU would live every moment as a new and fresh one—with nothing old attached to anything? What would that do to your new day and life? How will you live as brand-new in every brand-new split second?

Turning your what IFs into what IS!

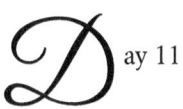ay 11

WHAT IF YOU would create more heart-touching moments for yourself and others? What happiness would that create? What loving experiences will you plan for today?

Turning your what IFs into what IS!

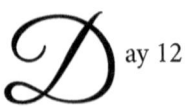 ay 12

WHAT IF YOU would play freely and without any worries? Would your experience of life change? How? What kind of playtime will you invest in, and with whom?

___

Turning your what IFs into what IS!

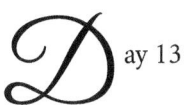ay 13

WHAT IF YOU would follow your heart's guidance, what your heart says? What wisdom would that bring? How will you follow your heart more often?

___

Turning your what IFs into what IS!

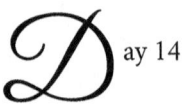 ay 14

WHAT IF YOU would take 100% responsibility for your feelings? Would it change how you feel? What clarity could this bring? How will you step into your power and take charge of all your emotions?

Turning your what IFs into what IS!

ay 15

WHAT IF YOU would show up as the big energy that you are? What would happen to your confidence? How will you make yourself big first before you start your new day, and also stay big?

_____
_____
_____
_____
_____
_____
_____
_____
_____
_____
_____
_____
_____
_____
_____
_____
_____
_____
_____
_____
_____
_____
_____

Turning your what IFs into what IS!

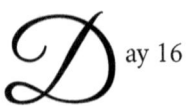ay 16

WHAT IF YOU would not budge on anything anymore, and instead, stay aligned with who you are? What would happen? How will you guarantee to be yourself unapologetically?

___

Turning your what IFs into what IS!

ay 17

WHAT IF YOU would say what you need very loud and clear? How would that change your confidence, and also your surroundings? What will you communicate with determination more often?

Turning your what IFs into what IS!

ay 18

WHAT IF YOU would not be afraid of anything? What would happen and how would that change you and your experience of life? What unnecessary frights will you give up?

Turning your what IFs into what IS!

ay 19

WHAT IF YOU would let go of all your unfitting and old beliefs? Would giving them up change how you behave? What new and well-feeling beliefs will you replace the old with?

___

Turning your what IFs into what IS!

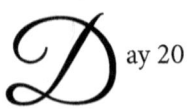ay 20

WHAT IF YOU would only eat clean food that you like, and only as much as you need? What would happen? How would that change your physical body? What fitting-for-you food will you indulge in?

Turning your what IFs into what IS!

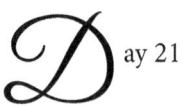 ay 21

WHAT IF YOU would BE and live the abundance that you naturally are? What would that change for you? How will you focus on all abundance?

Turning your what IFs into what IS!

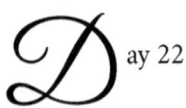 ay 22

WHAT IF YOU would treasure and celebrate your soul being - your inner you - every day? What would happen, what would change? How will you honor your inner gem today?

Turning your what IFs into what IS!

ay 23

WHAT IF YOU would stop minding the lives of other people? What would happen for you? What would change? How will you focus on yourself and your life?

Turning your what IFs into what IS!

Day 24

WHAT IF YOU would make your happiness a priority? Would it change how you live your life? How will you make your own joy and bliss an absolute must?

Turning your what IFs into what IS!

ay 25

WHAT IF YOU would stop judging yourself—and also quit judging others? What peaceful state would that create, for yourself and your surroundings? How will you refrain from judging?

Turning your what IFs into what IS!

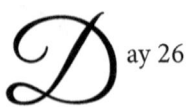 Day 26

WHAT IF YOU would aim for an adventurous life? What kind of experience would that be? How will you allow fun ventures in your journey?

Turning your what IFs into what IS!

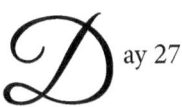 ay 27

WHAT IF YOU would move more—and create more movement in your life? What would that shift for you, your physical body, mind, soul, and consciousness? How will you move a lot more?

Turning your what IFs into what IS!

ay 28

WHAT IF YOU WOULD RELAX? What would happen? How will you relax more often?

___

Turning your what IFs into what IS!

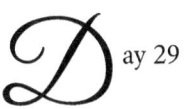 ay 29

WHAT IF YOU would be more flexible in every way? What change would that bring for your body, mind, soul, and consciousness? How will you be and stay flexible?

Turning your what IFs into what IS!

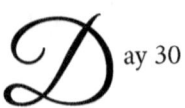 ay 30

WHAT IF YOU would be more open and allowing to leave all as-is? What energy would that create for yourself, others, and your surroundings? How will you give up the fight? What will you let be as-is?

Turning your what IFs into what IS!

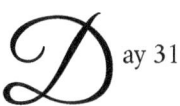ay 31

WHAT IF YOU would love everything and everyone, and commit to making this your lifestyle? What energy would that create for yourself and what changes would that bring to your life? How will you love more unconditionally?

___

Turning your what IFs into what IS!

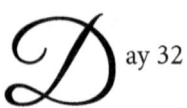 ay 32

WHAT IF YOU would BE and live deeply present in your NOW? What would happen for you? What feelings would come forward? How will you experience your NOW more consciously?

Turning your what IFs into what IS!

ay 33

WHAT IF YOU lay your past to rest by accepting it as part of yourself? What would that change for you? How would you live differently? What will you lay to rest?

___

Turning your what IFs into what IS!

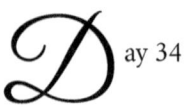 ay 34

WHAT IF YOU start imagining your future with pure excitement? How would that change your NOW and your future? How will you visualize more joy?

Turning your what IFs into what IS!

ay 35

WHAT IF YOU would BE and live your warrior essence? What would you do differently? How would you live your life? How will you activate your inner fighter, and let it live fully and vividly?

___

Turning your what IFs into what IS!

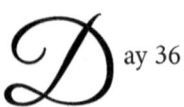 ay 36

WHAT IF YOU would be more grateful by focusing on being thankful all the time? What would change for you, your life, and others in your life? How will you show gratitude?

___

Turning your what IFs into what IS!

ay 37

WHAT IF YOU use your natural healing powers—physical, emotional, energetic, or spiritual? What would that initiate for you, others, and consciousness? How, when, and where will you administer your healer abilities?

Turning your what IFs into what IS!

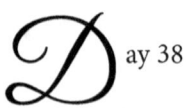ay 38

WHAT IF YOU respect everything and everyone? What would happen, for you and everything? How will you show respect to yourself and others, even if it's hard?

Turning your what IFs into what IS!

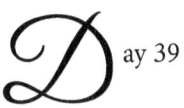ay 39

WHAT IF YOU would BE and live happier? What would happen for your body, mind, soul, and consciousness? What would this change? How will you BE and live with more joy?

___

Turning your what IS's into what IS!

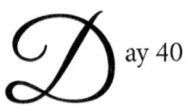# Day 40

WHAT IF YOU gave more praise to yourself and others? Would that change how you feel about yourself, and others? What unlimited bragging will you do—about yourself and others?

Turning your what IFs into what IS!

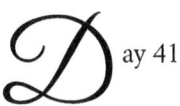ay 41

WHAT IF YOU make today your *best day ever*? What day would you have, how would you feel, and what would you create? How will you make sure that today is going to be the *best one ever*?

Turning your what IFs into what IS!

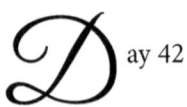ay 42

WHAT IF YOU go along with the energy of today's weather? What good energy will you latch onto, and what change will you observe in yourself because of that?

Turning your what IFs into what IS!

ay 43

WHAT IF YOU ask your body what it needs and when it needs it? How will that communication with your physicality change how you feel—physically, emotionally, energetically, or spiritually? How will you talk with your body uninterrupted?

_____
_____
_____
_____
_____
_____
_____
_____
_____
_____
_____
_____
_____
_____
_____
_____
_____
_____
_____
_____

Turning your what IFs into what IS!

ay 44

WHAT IF YOU would send love and light to everyone and everything consciously? What would happen for yourself and everything by doing so? How will you send this light and love?

Turning your what IFs into what IS!

ay 45

WHAT IF YOU drink enough water? What changes would that create for your wellbeing physically, mentally, and soulfully? How will you make sure to hydrate, and stay hydrated, with the fitting kind of water—still, bubbly, or naturally flavored?

Turning your what IFs into what IS!

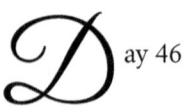 Day 46

WHAT IF YOU forgive everything and everyone—for everything? What would happen for you and what would change? How will you let go of all your trauma?

Turning your what IFs into what IS!

ay 47

WHAT IF YOU would start speaking your heart's truth? What loveliness and power would that spark? How will you be more truthful to who you are and speak more clearly about what fits?

___

Turning your what IFs into what IS!

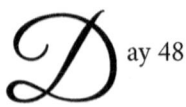 ay 48

WHAT IF YOU would see the world through the eyes of a child again? What would change in your outlook in life? What would you do differently or more often? How will you be more childlike again?

Turning your what IFs into what IS!

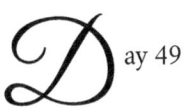 Day 49

WHAT IF YOU stop talking about anything negative, bad, ugly, or wrong? What would happen for you, your life, and your surroundings? How will you stop negativing?

___

Turning your what IFs into what IS!

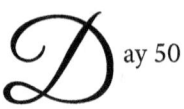ay 50

WHAT IF YOU would be kinder—to yourself and others? What life experience would that create for you and others? How will you BE and live a purer kindness?

Turning your what IFs into what IS!

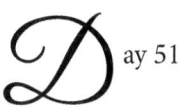 Day 51

WHAT IF YOU drench everything and everyone into your humungous love? What would happen? How would that change yourself, everything, and everyone? How will you BE and live the grand love that you are?

Turning your what IFs into what IS!

Day 52

WHAT IF YOU would see pure positive light everywhere, in everything, and in everyone? What would that mean for you? How will you see past the darkness, and instead see the light that is always there?

Turning your what IFs into what IS!

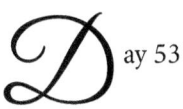 ay 53

WHAT IF YOU count your blessings more often? What would that mean for yourself and your life? How will you experience all the good that is there for you right now?

Turning your what IFs into what IS!

ay 54

WHAT IF YOU stop whatever you are doing to listen to the song birds—or to look at some sunshine, the moon and stars; the fresh scent of a flower? What shifts would that create for you and in your life? How will you make time for the little things today?

Turning your what IFs into what IS!

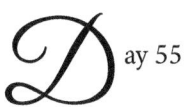 ay 55

WHAT IF YOU accept everything and everyone? What changes would that create? How will you accept yourself and everything more freely?

Turning your what IFs into what IS!

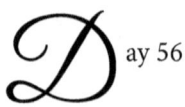 ay 56

WHAT IF YOU DREAM BIGGER? What would happen, and what would it change for you? Would this also bring change for others and your surroundings? How will you dream, bigger than gigantic, more often?

_____
_____
_____
_____
_____
_____
_____
_____
_____
_____
_____
_____
_____
_____
_____
_____
_____
_____
_____
_____
_____
_____
_____

Turning your what IFs into what IS!

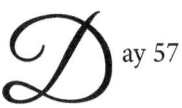ay 57

WHAT IF YOU think more positively? What would that do for you? How would your emotional, physical, and spiritual health be impacted? How will you think positive thoughts—and shift the negative to positive ones?

___

Turning your what IFs into what IS!

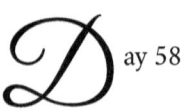 ay 58

WHAT IF YOU would thank everything and everyone at all times? What goodness would that create? How will you say and show a beautiful "Thank you!" more often?

___

Turning your what IFs into what IS!

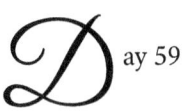Day 59

WHAT IF YOU let go of rules? What would happen? How would your life change? What rules will you let slide?

___

Turning your what IFs into what IS!

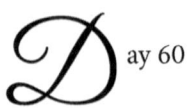 Day 60

WHAT IF YOU would give in to your passion? What changes would that bring? What feelings would you feel? How will you dive deeper into your passions to see where they lead you?

Turning your what IFs into what IS!

Day 61

WHAT IF YOU let your gifts shine? What creativity would that spark? How different would you feel? How will you show your unique capabilities with pride and glory?

Turning your what IPs into what IS!

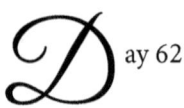ay 62

WHAT IF YOU would not be scared of death? Would that change the way you live your life? How will you live your life without being afraid to die?

Turning your what IFs into what IS!

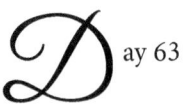 ay 63

WHAT IF YOU would admire yourself in the mirror all the time? Would that change how you feel about yourself? What self-love would that spark? How will you stare - fully in love with yourself - at yourself more often?

Turning your what IFs into what IS!

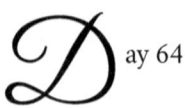# Day 64

WHAT IF YOU would let yourself be *yourself* ? What kind of life would you have? How much fun would there be? How will you let yourself be your true you?

Turning your what IFs into what IS!

ay 65

WHAT IF YOU embrace all your feelings and emotions? What would change for you and how you feel about yourself? How will you give every feeling and emotion its rightful space?

___

Turning your what IFs into what IS!

ay 66

WHAT IF YOU would step outside of your comfort box—and your normal way of living? How would you experience your life? How different would you be from your normal you? How will you break past your glass ceiling?

Turning your what IFs into what IS!

ay 67

WHAT IF YOU would show your true colors? What would happen for you, your life, and your future ? How will you show your unique you?

___

Turning your what IFs into what IS!

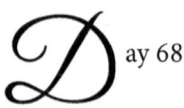ay 68

WHAT IF YOU would serve yourself, and others, more often and with a full heart? What would that do for you, them, and the world? How will you serve compassionately?

Turning your what IFs into what IS!

ay 69

WHAT IF YOU would leave any and all drama alone? What would that do to your life and your sanity? How will you steer clear of all gossip and craziness?

Turning your what IFs into what IS!

Day 70

WHAT IF YOU would be more generous? How would that change your personality and your life—your future? How will you be more giving to yourself and others?

Turning your what IFs into what IS!

ay 71

WHAT IF YOU notice all the little messages more consciously? What different kind of life would you have? What guidance would BE there? How will you see, hear, taste, smell, feel, and think of these little messages that are always there for you?

___

Turning your what IFs into what IS!

ay 72

WHAT IF YOU would think of the impossible as very possible? What would happen? How would you live your life differently? How will you change your way of thinking from "not doable" to "absolutely doable?"

___

Turning your what IFs into what IS!

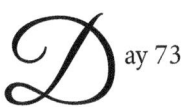 ay 73

WHAT IF YOU would just go for it—whatever "it" is? What would happen? How much more fun would life be? How will you let yourself go for what it is that you want so dearly?

Turning your what ITs into what IS!

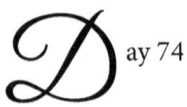

Day 74

WHAT IF YOU would show up as the best version of you possible—the happiest, most well-feeling, and ultimately positive? What change would that bring for yourself and your life—your NOW and your future? How will you make sure to be the most phenomenal you ever?

Turning your what IFs into what IS!

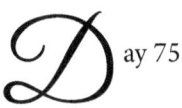ay 75

WHAT IF YOU would let yourself rest until you are rested—let yourself do nothing more often? What wellness would that initiate in your whole being—body, mind, soul, consciousness? How will you allow and create more quiet moments for yourself?

Turning your what IFs into what IS!

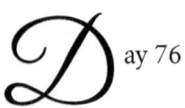 Day 76

WHAT IF YOU would eat cleaner food? What would happen; for your body, mind, soul, and life? How will you eat better, and more of what your body needs?

Turning your what IFs into what IS!

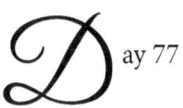 ay 77

WHAT IF YOU appreciate everything and everyone? What does that mean for you, others, and your surroundings? How will you appreciate the whole world, and all that's in life?

___

Turning your what IFs into what IS!

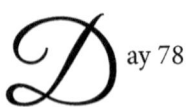 ay 78

WHAT IF YOU would connect to consciousness - the one-ness that we all are - more often? What would change with such a focused practice? How will you feel yourself being ONE with all?

Turning your what IFs into what IS!

ay 79

WHAT IF YOU would be aligned with the biggest part of you—the energetic essence, your soul being, your inner you? What difference would that make in your experience of life? How will you align, align, again, again, and again?

Turning your what IFs into what IS!

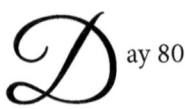 ay 80

WHAT IF YOU would feel deserving? What changes would that initiate for you and your life? How will you recognize yourself as deserving for all the good in life?

Turning your what IFs into what IS!

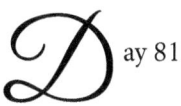 Day 81

WHAT IF YOU stop restricting yourself and others with sayings like, "Life is hard" and "Suffering is normal" or "You can't have everything you want?" What would change for yourself and others? How will you turn these old untrue beliefs into new and true habits?

Turning your what IFs into what IS!

ay 82

WHAT IF YOU would take every chance there is to laugh out loud? How would your life change? What would this do to your overall health? How will you take these chances, and not let one slip away?

Turning your what IFs into what IS!

ay 83

WHAT IF YOU would give yourself, everyone, and everything a chance—no matter the what, when, or how? What would change in your life and those of other people? How will you give fair chances without limitations—like air that gives oxygen without restrictions?

Turning your what IFs into what IS!

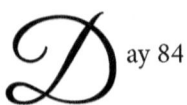 ay 84

WHAT IF YOU put more emphasis on living simpler? What would change? What energy would that create? How will you simplify your life?

Turning your what IFs into what IS!

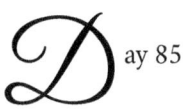 ay 85

WHAT IF YOU COMPLAIN LESS? What would happen? How will you stop complaining?

Turning your what ITs into what IS!

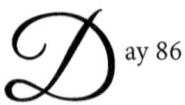 ay 86

WHAT IF YOU would refrain from making a happening about yourself when it's actually about someone else? What difference would that make in your life? How will you stay out of other people's business, and instead experience their happenings as a spectator?

Turning your what IFs into what IS!

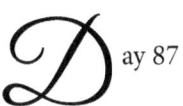 ay 87

WHAT IF YOU would go for spontaneity in life? What coolness would that mean for you and your adventure of being alive? How will you BE and live, and also stay, free spirited?

Turning your what IFs into what IS!

Day 88

WHAT IF YOU would not take everything and everyone so seriously? Would that change how you live your life? How will you stay light-hearted—and not take everything so gravely?

Turning your what IFs into what IS!

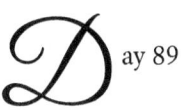 Day 89

WHAT IF YOU would pretend to be a super star? How would that change your life? How will you BE and live in that super-star energy?

Turning your what IFs into what IS!

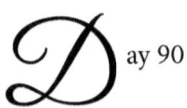 ay 90

WHAT IF YOU would have a super power? What would it be and how would it change your life? How will you use your super power?

___

Turning your what IFs into what IS!

* * *

Ready to continue on your self-growth path? Get the next journal in this series: ***Open - Where it all starts!***

BONUS

Because hey, nobody ever wants the goodness to end.

Keep going!

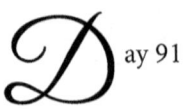Day 91

WHAT IF YOU would become best friends with all your physical and emotional symptoms; your problems, issues, hardships, and traumas? What would happen to how you see and feel about them? What change would that bring for your life? How will you love all of you - and your whole life - anyway and no matter what?

Turning your what IFs into what IS!

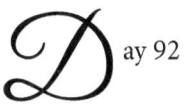 Day 92

WHAT IF YOU would understand that you can have anything that you want? Would that change you, your life, and how you live you life? How will you trust the knowing that you can have whatever you want?

Turning your what IFs into what IS!

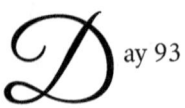# Day 93

WHAT IF YOU would BE and live in a high-for-life frequency no matter the circumstances? How different would your life be? How will you BE and live happy as can be, on top of the mountain, no matter what?

___

Turning your what IFs into what IS!

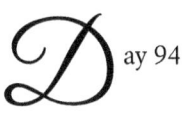 ay 94

WHAT IF YOU would not pay any attention to the nay-sayers, the negativers, and the downers? What would happen? How would you experience your life differently? How will you stay clear from all that nonsense?

___

Turning your what IFs into what IS!

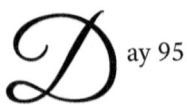 Day 95

WHAT IF YOU would live like nobody's watching—not caring what others think or say about you, or expect of you? How would you live differently? What feelings would that create for you? How will you make sure to live your life fully and vividly?

Turning your what IFs into what IS!

AND NOW IT'S YOUR TURN!

The following are your magical pages to turn your own personal what ifs into what IS.

I'm counting on you to go big here!

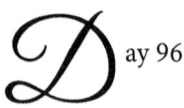 Day 96

WHAT IF...

Turning your what IFs into what IS!

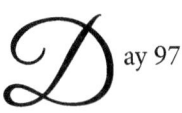ay 97

WHAT IF...

Turning your what IFs into what IS!

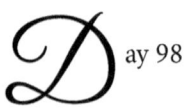 ay 98

WHAT IF...

Turning your what IFs into what IS!

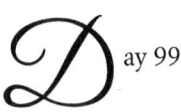 ay 99

WHAT IF…

Turning your what IFs into what IS!

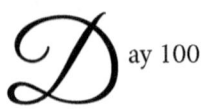 Day 100

WHAT IF...

Turning your what IFs into what IS!

ALSO BY JACQUELINE PIRTLE

365 Days of Happiness

Because happiness is a piece of cake!

This passage book invites you to create a daily habit to live your every day joy, and is the parent companion to ***365 Days of Happiness***, the journal workbook.

* * *

365 Days of Happiness - Special Edition

Because happiness is a piece of cake

This beautiful Special Edition of the bestseller ***365 Days of Happiness: Because happiness is a piece of cake*** has room for your notes after every daily passage.

* * *

365 Days of Happiness - Journal Workbook

This enlightening journal workbook is your daily tool to create a habit of living your every day bliss, and is the companion to ***365 Days of Happiness: Because happiness is a piece of cake***.

* * *

Life IS Beautiful - Here's to New Beginnings

If you like digging deeper into the meaning of life and are inspired by spirituality, then you'll love Jacqueline's effective teachings.

* * *

Parenting Through the Eyes of Lollipops

A Guide to Conscious Parenting

If you like harmony at home and laughter in the house, then you'll love Jacqueline's inspirational methods.

* * *

What it Means to BE a Woman

And Yes! Women do Poop!

If you like to live free, empowered, and want to decide for yourself, then you'll love Jacqueline's liberating ways.

* * *

Open - A 30 Day Journal

Turning your what IFs into it IS!

If you like to be open to live your life fully, allow your dreams to come true, enjoy journaling, and want to squeeze the most out of your time, then you'll love Jacqueline Pirtle's uplifting teachings.

* * *

Open - A 90 Day Journal - The Extended Edition

Turning your what IFs into it IS!

If you like to be open to live your life fully, allow your dreams to come true, enjoy journaling, and want to squeeze the most out of your time, then you'll love Jacqueline Pirtle's uplifting teachings.

ABOUT THE AUTHOR

Bestselling author, podcaster, and holistic practitioner, Jacqueline Pirtle, has twenty-four years of experience helping thousands of clients discover their own happiness. Jacqueline is the owner of *FreakyHealer* and has shared her solid teachings through her podcast **The Daily Freak**, sessions, workshops, presentations, and books with clients all over the world. She holds international degrees in holistic health and natural living. Her effective healing work has been featured in print and online magazines, podcasts, radio shows, on TV, and in the documentary *The Overly Emotional Child by Learning Success*, available on Amazon Prime.

For any questions you might have, to sign up for Jacqueline's newsletter, and for more information on whatever else she is up to, visit www.freakyhealer.com and her social media accounts @freakyhealer.

www.ingramcontent.com/pod-product-compliance
Lightning Source LLC
Chambersburg PA
CBHW071420070526
44578CB00003B/631